Japanese mythology for beginners

Experience the exciting sagas of Japan and discover step by step the culture of the country Japan

Tobias Kuhn

CONTENT

What you can expect in this book.................1

Basics.................4

  Shintō.................4

  Japanese mythology cosmos.................7

The mythological narrative 10

  Kuniumi and Kamiumi 10

  Mihashira no Uzu no Miko 16

  Susanoo and Ōkuninushi.................20

  Kuniyuzuri and Tenson kōrin 24

  Jinmu.................27

Meaning 30

  Explanation of natural and cultural phenomena 30

  Role and (Pseudo) Historicity of the Tennō...... 34

  Motifs.................38

Source 42

  Kojiki 42

  Nihon shoki 46

Other mythologies within Japan 49

  Buddhist-Shintōist Syncretism 49

  Mythology of the Ainu 52

Folk tales and urban legends 54

What you can ex-pect in this book

From a European-Western perspective, much of what is related to the state of Japan, including its history and culture and the people who live there, seems not only foreign, but also in some ways inaccessible and incomprehensible. Those who do not deal with it explicitly often have no connection to Japan at all. This, of course, is also true of Japanese mythology. In contrast to Greco-Roman or Nordic-Germanic mythology, the level of knowledge about it in the West is rather low. The enormous geographical and cultural distance ensures that it is rather unlikely to have one or even several people in the immediate vicinity who are familiar with this topic. In other words, it is a niche interest in this country. Are you interested in filling one or the other educational gap in this direction? Maybe you already have some basic knowledge about Japan and would like to deal with the mythology there next, or you are generally interested in how the imprint of different cultures around the world is expressed by their respective mythologies.

In each of these cases, you have made the right decision in buying this book. The cultural peculiarities of the world are diverse and each of them is exciting in itself and offers the observer a lot of interesting things. Japan is no exception. And that is what this book is about.

Since the content of this book is aimed at beginners, I will refrain from going into too much incidental detail and from giving details that are relevant only to professional Japanologists. Since I will translate speaking names and explain historical backgrounds and contexts, knowledge of Japanese language or history is in no way assumed. Instead, this book is intended to give non-specialist readers an overview of the whole range of topics related to the keyword "Japanese mythology." This includes by far not only the myths and legends themselves. You will learn everything about basic concepts that are indispensable for dealing with the subject. Against what background Japanese mythology is to be considered, what the mythological tales are about, how they are interpreted, in which literary works they are primarily recorded and much more.

Basics

SHINTŌ

Although Japan no longer has an officially defined state religion since the complete secularization imposed on the country's government by the American occupation in 1945 after the end of World War II, there are nevertheless two faiths that are by far the most popular and most strongly represented among the Japanese population: One is Buddhism, more specifically its Japanese manifestation, which differs from those found on the Asian mainland, and the other is Shintō (also known in non-specialist circles by the less accurate name "Shintōism").

You may have noticed that I have deliberately used the term "faiths" instead of "religions" here. On this question of whether Shintō is a religion at all, or whether Shintō should be referred to as such in humanities literature and treated accordingly, there is no unambiguously correct answer even within Japanology; opinions differ in this regard.

But it is not only in Japanese studies in general that difficulties arise with the definition of Shintō. For this book in particular, the position of Shintō in Japan also makes it difficult in places to delineate what should and should not be counted as Japanese mythology. Most mythological narratives that can be described as Shintōistic are so inextricably linked to everyday Japanese life that a distinction between Japanese mythology and Shintō mythology is often not discernible.

Just like Japanese traditions and Shintō traditions, the two concepts are often to be regarded as almost identical, so that it is difficult or sometimes simply impossible to classify a certain phenomenon as exclusively Japanese or Shintōistic, because characteristic Japanese peculiarities are usually of Shintōistic origin or at least strongly related to Shintō. By virtue of the fact that almost every cultural tradition in Japanese intellectual history is influenced in some way by Shintōistic elements, it would be possible and legitimate to treat them all as a collective mythology. However, it would be highly confusing and unwieldy, especially for a beginner, to attempt to deal with all of this content at once. To be overwhelmed by such a vast amount of information, such as names, stories, and concepts, would be rather daunting and thus anything but conducive to engagement with the subject.

For this reason, I have chosen to focus on what might be broadly defined as "pure" Shintō mythology. I will deal with everything related to it first and only briefly discuss other mythological ideas at the end.

JAPANESE MYTHOLOGY COSMOS

In advance, some short definitions of terms are also necessary. In Japanese mythology, the kami are mentioned at absolutely all times. The Japanese word "kami" often becomes "god/gods" in translations of Japanese-language texts into Western languages. While this translation is appropriate in some cases, depending on the text, translations such as "soul/s," "nature spirit/s," "essence/s," or "holiness" are also possible in Japanese usage. In the context of Shintō, all of these meanings apply in some sense. Moreover, kami are not only existences of supernatural or otherworldly origin, but also deceased ancestors or rulers. It also happens that plants, objects or even individual parts of other kami are understood as kami. Since there is no German word that combines all these meanings and thus really has exactly the same connotations, I will use the Japanese term untranslated.

Furthermore, to understand it is beneficial to understand how the world is constructed according to Japanese mythology. It is composed of the sky, called Takamagahara (literally "high level of the sky"), and the earth. Where exactly heaven is located is never mentioned in detail. It is possible that the actual sky is meant, but there are also interpretations according to which the mythology refers to places in Japan that are far away and distant from human civilization, mainly mountains.

Heaven and earth are separated from each other and connected by a free-floating bridge called Ama no Ukihashi (literally "floating bridge of heaven"). Below the earth lies the underworld or world of the dead, Yomi (the etymological origin of the word is not known, which is why it is rather to be understood as a proper name without meaning), to which all the deceased go, regardless of their way of life. In addition, there exists another place also often referred to as the underworld in Western translations called Ne no Kuni (literally "root land"). Depending on the tradition, this place is either identical with the underworld called Yomi or it is another lower world, a realm of the dead, from which life blossoms anew. If in the following the underworld is spoken of, Yomi is always meant, the root country is always named as such for the sake of unambiguity.

In the beginning, most of the kami live in heaven and enter the earth only temporarily, if at all, before they return to heaven, die, and thus enter the underworld or "retire," which usually just means that they no longer appear in the narrative from that point on. Later, several kami live on earth and are demarcated from those in heaven.

Japan, of course, is located on Earth. Since the Japanese state did not yet exist under this name and in its modern form at the time of the mythology's origin, the group of islands that make up present-day Japan is given different names in myths created at different times. Partly these are very poetic paraphrases, such as Ashihara no Nakatsukuni (literally "land within the reed plains") or Toyoashihara no Mizuho no Kuni (literally "land of young rice ears on the rich reed plains"), but partly they are the names of former provinces within Japan, sometimes used as synonyms for the whole of Japan or for the whole world. This is because many local tales and anecdotes have been incorporated into the all-Japan mythology over time, and these tales often mention only the name of their place of origin when referring to the human world. The historical province of Izumo, which was located in the eastern part of what is now Shimane Prefecture, is mentioned particularly frequently.

The mythological narrative

KUNIUMI AND KAMIUMI

The narrative of Japanese mythology begins with the creation of the universe. The cause of this emergence is not specified and at the beginning the universe is in a chaotic, formless state. At about the same time, five generations of kami, called the Koto Amatsukami (literally "distinguished celestial kami"), arise out of nothing. The heaven and the earth arise and separate from each other.

Thus, the earth already exists, but consists only of sea and has no land yet. After the creation of heaven and earth, seven more generations, the so-called Kamiyo Nanayo (literally "seven generations of the age of kami"), are added. While the five generations of the Koto Amatsukami and the first two generations of the Kamiyo Nanayo each consist of only one sexless kami, which has appeared spontaneously and does not reproduce, the later five generations of the Kamiyo Nanayo are each composed of two siblings, a male and a female kami, who together bring the next generation into being.

This is followed by the era known as Kuniumi (literally "birth of the land"), in which the beginning of the existence of our world is to be classified. The myth speaks of the two kami Izanagi no Mikoto (literally "the inviter"; hereafter Izanagi) and Izanami no Mikoto (literally "the inviter"; in f. Izanami), who, as the seventh and last generation of the Kamiyo Nanayo, are both siblings and a pair. From their predecessors, they are given the responsibility over creating the land. They enter the bridge that connects heaven and earth. From there, they create the first land mass in history by touching the surface of the water with a jeweled spear, stirring the water, and then lifting the spear above the water so that some drops of salt water fall back onto the surface of the water, becoming Onogoroshima Island (literally, "island coagulated by itself").

Izanagi and Izanami enter this land themselves, build a palace supported by a pillar of heaven and marry there. Due to a mistake in the course of the wedding ritual, their first child, a son, is born imperfect. He is, depending on the source, either just walking disabled or has no arms and legs or even no bones. Because of this characteristic appearance, they call him Hiruko (literally "leech child") and abandon him on a small boat at sea.

After Izanagi and Izanami seek advice from the other kami still in heaven, they repeat the ceremony the right way and Izanami gives birth to most of the islands of Japan one after another, completing the Kuniumi and paving the way for the so-called Kamiumi (literally "birth of the kami").

Following the Japanese islands, Izanami also gives birth to numerous kami. Various sources speak of numbers between 800 and 800 million. The last of her children is Hi no Kagutsuchi (literally "shining power"; i. F. Kagutsuchi), the kami of fire. Depending on the lore, Kagutsuchi's body is either made entirely of flames or he constantly emits fire, which is why he inflicts such severe injuries on his mother during childbirth that she dies from them and must be buried. In his rage, Izanagi kills his son Kagutsuchi. From his remains, more kami are created and when Izanagi cuts his body into eight pieces with a sword, they become eight volcanoes.

Izanagi, driven by the desire to see his wife again, goes to the underworld, where he finally finds her. She expresses the wish that he not look at her, since she has already eaten of the fruits of the underworld and has been changed by them. When he disregards this request and tries to sneak a peek at the sleeping Izanami at night, he is horrified to discover that her once beautiful outer appearance has become that of a rotting and corroded corpse.

His scream wakes Izanami and Izanagi, pursued by her and a horde of warriors, flees from the underworld, which he succeeds in doing with the help of three peaches from a nearby tree. Arriving at the entrance to the underworld, his gaze and Izanami's meet for the last time before he closes the entrance with the help of a rock. In revenge, Izanami vows to let 1000 people die every day, whereupon Izanagi swears to ensure 1500 births every day.

Having been in the underworld and seeing the state Izanami was in, Izanagi performs a ritual of purification in a river. From his discarded clothes, as well as washing away the impurities from the underworld with the river water, several kami are created. Among these, the last three are particularly important to mention: The kami of the sun, Amaterasu-Ōmikami (literally "illuminating the sky"; i. F. Amaterasu), born from Izanagi's left eye; the kami of the moon, Tsukuyomi no Mikoto (literally "counting the moons resp. Tsukuyomi), born from his right eye; and the kami of the storm and the sea, Susanoo no Mikoto (literally, "the impetuous one"; i.e., Susanoo), born from his nose.

These three siblings are born at the same time and play probably the most important role in all of Japanese mythology. In a variation of the tale as rendered in the Nihonshoki, Amaterasu, Tsukuyomi and Susanoo are not created by Izanagi alone, but are three of the children that Izanagi and Izanami fathered together after their arrival on the newly created land. Amaterasu is their first child. In this tradition, Izanami does not die, which is why neither she nor her husband enter the underworld.

Before he retires, Izanagi divides the world between the three children: Amaterasu is given dominion over the sky, Tsukuyomi over the night, and Susanoo over the seas. Unlike his two siblings, Susanoo refuses to fulfill his task, preferring to be with Izanami. After crying for so long that he has already grown up and grown a beard eight handbreadths long, causing all the rivers to dry up in the meantime, he is banished to the Root Land by his father, who is not mentioned further from then on. This represents the end of the Kamiumi.

MIHASHIRA NO UZU NO MIKO

Amaterasu, Tsukuyomi and Susanoo are collectively known as Mihashira no Uzu no Miko (literally "the three noble or precious children"). Amaterasu, in particular, represents the central figure of Japanese mythology. In contrast to Tsukuyomi's importance is the small amount of mention in mythological texts. In fact, so little is known about Tsukuyomi that not even his or her gender is known. Mostly, however, it is assumed that he is a male kami.

Amaterasu and Tsukuyomi marry and temporarily share heaven. When Amaterasu sends Tsukuyomi as her representative to Ukemochi, kami of food and another daughter of Izanagi and Izanami, Tsukuyomi kills Ukemochi out of disgust that she creates food from various parts of her body. More kami are also created from her remains. Amaterasu and Tsukuyomi separate, and the deeply angry Amaterasu decides that she never wants to see Tsukuyomi again.

Before Susanoo begins his exile, he ascends to his sister Amaterasu in the sky to say goodbye to her. In order to prove to her that his intentions are sincere, the two siblings engage in a contest, the exact course of which varies from source to source. During this contest, many more kami are created from the clothing, jewelry, weapons, and other items that the two siblings carry with them. At this point, however, only Ame no Oshihomimi should be mentioned, which was created from the jewels that Amaterasu had worn in her hair.

After the end of the contest, Susanoo commits a series of sacrilegious misdeeds called amatsutsumi (literally "heavenly crimes or sins"), including destroying crops, desecrating sacred places, and angering and even mortally wounding other kami. Depending on the source, he does this either because he loses the contest and is frustrated by it, or because he wins it and is so intoxicated by his victory that he can no longer control his own behavior.

Amaterasu is initially still willing to overlook Susanoo's deeds, but after he finally skins a horse, punctures the roof of Amaterasu's weaving hall, throws the skinned horse through one of the holes into the interior of the hall and thus mortally wounds one of the weavers, she too has finally had enough. She retreats in horror into a cave, and since she embodies the sun, the sunlight disappears from the sky and the earth, leaving her in darkness.

Led by Tokoyo no Omoikane (literally "eternally serving his thoughts"), the kami of wisdom, the other kami devise a plan to persuade Amaterasu to return with the help of a spectacular performance outside the cave. The performance includes singing birds and uprooted trees. Its most important part consists of a ritualistic, pantomimic dance performed by Ame no Uzume no Mikoto (i. F. Ame no Uzume), kami of twilight, gaiety and art, in a kind of trance state in front of the cave. In doing so, she offers a comical, entertaining sight dressed in flowers, leaves, and plants before removing her clothes and performing the dance naked.

Thus, she manages to make all the gathered kami laugh out loud, which Amaterasu also witnesses in the cave. When she looks outside, she sees herself in a mirror that was previously placed in front of the entrance. She walks towards the mirror and is blinded by her own brightly shining reflection, so she does not recognize herself at first. The kami Ame no Tajikarao (literally "strong hand of heaven"), standing by the entrance, seizes the opportunity and pulls her out of the cave entirely. After being implored and desperately begged to return by the other kami, she agrees and the light of the sun returns to the world. The scene in which she leaves the cave, faces the performance of

Ame no Uzume and the other kami, and allows the sunlight to shine again is one of the most famous moments in Japanese mythology and has been artistically immortalized many times. Susanoo is subjected to a purification ceremony as punishment for his actions and is banished once again.

SUSANOO AND ŌKUNINUSHI

Susanoo, who has been banished to earth, meets a grieving old couple who tell him that in the last seven years seven of their eight daughters have been eaten by Yamata no Orochi (literally "eight-forked giant snake"; i. F. Orochi), a giant snake- or dragon-like monster with eight heads and eight tails. As the time approaches for Orochi to appear for the eighth time and also take their last daughter, Kushinada-hime (literally "wondrous princess of the rice fields"), they ask Susanoo for help.

This one reveals himself as Amaterasu's brother and offers to kill Orochi if they allow him to marry their daughter. He transforms Kushinada-hime into a comb and hides her in his hair from the monster. The couple then brews sake at Susanoo's instruction, with which Orochi is made drunk and then killed by Susanoo. In the body of the monster he finds the legendary sword Kusanagi no Tsurugi (literally "grass-cutting sword"), which he presents as a gift to his sister Amaterasu upon his return to make up for his behavior and settle the dispute between the two siblings.

Ōkuninushi no Mikoto (wörtlich „Besitzer bzw. Meister des großen Landes"; i. F. Ōkuninushi), der je nach Quelle entweder ein Sohn oder ein Urururururenkel (d. h. Nachfahre in sechster Generation) von Susanoo und Kushinada-hime ist, reist mit seinen 80 älteren Brüdern bzw. He travels to a foreign kingdom with his 80 older brothers or half-brothers (the number 80 is possibly not meant literally and can also stand for a very large number), as they are all interested in the princess Yagami-hime who lives there. The brothers go ahead and encounter a wounded rabbit that has been attacked by crocodiles and sharks and needs help.

In their cruel nature, they play a trick on him so that his pain and suffering become even worse. Ōkuninushi, who is following them, also meets the rabbit and helps him. Because of his helpfulness, he attracts the attention of Princess Yagami-hime, which earns him the envy of his brothers. Together, the jealous brothers lure Ōkuninushi into a trap so that he burns himself to death on a red-hot rock. His mother asks Kamimusubi no Mikoto (literally "Kami bringing forth"), one of the Koto Amatsukami mentioned above, to bring him back to life. The latter grants her wish and Ōkuninushi is restored as a handsome young man.

Afterwards the process repeats itself, the brothers kill him again by splitting a tree with a wedge and making it snap back together, crushing Ōkuninushi. His mother again succeeds in bringing him back. This time, she then advises him to flee to the root country to Susanoo. During his escape, he narrowly escapes a third and final attempt on his life by his brothers.

After the successful escape, he seeks out Susanoo and falls in love with his daughter, Suseri-hime. Susanoo does not agree to a marriage of the two, so he sets him four tests, which are designed by their absurd difficulty not to be passed. After passing them anyway - three of them thanks to the help of Suseri-hime and one thanks to the help of a field mouse - he ties Susanoo's hair to the girders of the palace roof and escapes with Suseri-hime as well as Susanoo's sword, his bow and his koto (Japanese zither). When he accidentally strikes a tree with the koto, Susanoo wakes up, accidentally knocks down the girders by stomping on them too quickly and violently, and in this way brings down his own palace. He pursues them to the entrance of the Root Land despite their head start. However, by passing the tests and making a spectacular escape, Ōkuninushi had managed to impress Susanoo in the meantime.

Instead of pursuing the two lovers, he gives them his blessing and leaves Ōkuninushi his weapons, with which he succeeds in defeating his brothers after their return and becomes master of the earthly realm. At the same time, he re-forms the land, which is considered a continuation of the act of creation that was interrupted by Izanami's death.

KUNIYUZURI AND TENSON KŌRIN

Amaterasu offers her son Ame no Oshihomimi to rule the earth. Since he refuses, on the grounds that in his estimation the earth is still too wild and untamed, Amaterasu makes the same offer to her second son, Ame no Hohi. The latter sets off, but once on Earth, he and the Ōkuninushi, who rules over Earth, develop mutual sympathies, so Ame no Hohi is no longer interested in taking over and no longer reports back to his mother. His son, Ame no Wakahiko, is the next to receive Amaterasu's offer and is sent to Earth. However, there he marries Ōkuninushi's daughter, Shitateruhime, and also disregards his original assignment. Because of this, Amaterasu and Takamimusubi no Mikoto (literally, "high-souled one who brings forth"), another Koto Amatsukami, send the kami of thunder and sword, Takemikazuchi (literally, about "brave lightning and thunder"), who is one of the kami created at Kagutsuchi's assassination by Izanagi, to subjugate the land.

Upon his arrival, Takemikazuchi demands that Ōkuninushi hand over the land. Ōkuninushi leaves the decision to his two sons. While one of them, Yae

Kotoshironushi, immediately agrees to give him the land, the other, Takeminakata, challenges him to a fight, which Takemikazuchi wins. This process is called kuniyuzuri (literally "land surrender").

After subduing the land in this way, Amaterasu again offers Ame no Oshihomimi to rule over it. The latter instead proposes his son, Amatsuhiko Hikoho no Ninigi no Mikoto (i. F. Ninigi) as ruler, which Amaterasu and Takamimusubi accept. Ninigi enters the earth, being either alone or accompanied by other kami, depending on the tradition. His path to earth is referred to as Tenson kōrin (literally "descent from heaven"). Sarutahiko Ōkami (literally "prince of the monkey field," i. F. Sarutahiko), leader of the earthly kami, stands in his way, but is persuaded to let him pass by Ame no Uzume, mentioned earlier. Ame no Uzume and Sarutahiko become a couple. On earth, Ninigi falls in love with Konohanasakuya-hime (literally "princess of the blossoming cherry tree flowers"), kami of Mount Fuji. He asks her father, Ōyamatsumi (literally "dwelling in the great mountains"), kami of mountains and war, to marry her.

Ōyamatsumi offers him his older daughter, Iwanaga-hime, instead, whom Ninigi rejects because of her looks. Ōyamatsumi allows the marriage between

Ninigi and Konohanasakuya-hime, but curses Ninigi for rejecting Iwanaga-hime. As a result of the curse, Ninigi and all his descendants were deprived of immortality and their lifespans were drastically shortened. In other traditions, Iwanaga-hime herself is the one who pronounces the curse.

JINMU

Ninigi bequeaths a fishhook to his eldest son Hoderi no Mikoto (literally "glow of fire"; i. F. Hoderi) to make him a fisherman, and a bow to his younger brother Ho-ori no Mikoto (literally "wealth of harvest"; i. F. Hoori) to make him a hunter. Hoderi is unhappy with his gift, since a bow can be used in any weather, whereas fishing depends on the right weather. Since he is the older brother, he feels he deserves the more useful gift and persuades Hoori to trade. However, after he keeps missing his target with the bow, he wants to reverse the exchange. Hoori, however, loses the fishhook at sea. After Hoderi insists that he find it again and even threatens him with death, Hoori sets out to search in the sea. He meets Toyotama-hime (literally "Princess of Rich Jewels"), the daughter of Watatsumi (literally "Protector of the Sea"), the dragon-like kami of the water, whom he marries.

He then spends some time in Watatsumi's palace. After he tells his father-in-law about his situation, he has all the fish search for the hook. Finally, it is found in the mouth of a fish. Homesick Hoori returns to his brother with his wife, the hook cursed by Watatsumi, and a jewel that controls the tide and one that controls the flood. Hoderi realizes that he can no longer succeed with the hook because of the curse and attacks Hoori. The latter overpowers him with the help of the two jewels and Hoderi vows that his descendants will serve as bodyguards to those of Hoori.

Toyotama-hime becomes pregnant by Hoori. He builds a birthing hut for her out of cormorant feathers. As the birth of the child approaches, the hut is not yet completely finished and thus not opaque. Therefore, Toyotama-hime asks her husband not to look at her when the child is born, as she must assume her non-human form to do so. He is unable to restrain his curiosity and sees that she has transformed into a crocodile or shark-like dragon for the birth. Hoori is frightened and runs away.

Toyotama-hime is so ashamed that she retreats to the sea, leaving her husband and newborn son Ugayafukiaezu no Mikoto (literally "incomplete cormorant feather covering"; i. F. Ugayafukiaezu) behind and closing the path to the realm of the sea. She sends her younger sister Tamayori-hime to take care of the child. In other versions, Tamayori-hime has already come with them when Hoori and Toyotama-hime return. When Ugayafukiaezu grows up, he marries his aunt Tamayori-hime.

Together Ugayafukiaezu and Tamayori-hime have four sons. At the age of 45, their youngest son Kamu-yamato Iware-biko no Mikoto (i. F. Kamu-yamato I-ware-biko) advises his three brothers to migrate further east to learn more about the unexplored territories there and to find a more suitable place to administer the entire country. When they arrive after several years, Kamu-yamato Iware-biko is the only one among them still alive, his brothers having been killed in battles along the way. A three-legged crow leads him to what later becomes Yamato Province. Another man named Nigihayahi also claims the throne there, as he too claims descent from the kami. However, when he sees Kamu-yamato Iware-biko, he recognizes him as legitimate and voluntarily leaves the rule to him. Kamu-yamato Iware-biko then ascended the throne in 660 BC under the name Jinmu-Tennō, becoming the first emperor of Japan. With him and the dynasty he established, the age of kami ends and the age of humans, or human emperors, begins. He is said to have died in 585 BC at the age of 126.

Meaning

EXPLANATION OF NATURAL AND CULTURAL PHENOMENA

Many elements of Japanese mythology function as a kind of explanation of various phenomena observable in nature and Japanese culture. The closing of the entrance to the underworld by Izanagi establishes the fact that there is a separation and demarcation between the world of the living and the world of the dead that cannot be easily crossed.

Izanami's vow to ensure the birth of 1000 dead every day and Izanagi's reaction to this, to allow 1500 people to be born every day, sets in motion the beginning of the natural cycle of life and death. The natural alternation of day and night, or of sun and moon, is also explained mythologically: because Amaterasu and

Tsukuyomi are at odds and Amaterasu no longer wants to see Tsukuyomi, the sun and moon cannot be seen together. The cursing of Ninigi by Ōyamatsumi or Iwanaga-hime explains why human life has its average length. Even the simple fact that humans prepare food and eat it to survive has a mythological explanation. After Ukemochi's murder by Tsukuyomi, Amaterasu had the food she created brought to her, liked it, and decided that in the future it should also serve as food for the descendants of the kami.

The performance of Ame no Uzume in front of the cave is considered to be the mythological origin or inspiration for Japanese kagura theater, while the fight between Takemikazuchi and Takeminakata for dominion over the land is said to have represented Japan's first Sumō wrestling match, from which the traditional fights are inspired.

Japan's close relationship with the sea, which has always been important in the history of the country and its people, also goes back to mythology. There, the sea often functions as a kind of "other world" in which many of the laws that apply on land seem to be suspended. For example, it is written about the Palace of Watatsumi (Ryūgū-jō) that time passes differently there, or that there is a different season on each of its four sides. In earlier times, it still seems easy to travel between land and sea, but after the clearer separation between the two realms brought about by Toyotama-hime, this changes, which explains why it is not always easy to travel back and forth between land and sea without further ado. Hiruko, the son abandoned by Izanagi and Izanami, on the other hand, serves as an explanation for some positive attributes associated with the sea.

For example, the Japanese are usually extremely grateful for fish and other riches that wash ashore. Certain stones washed ashore are said to augur a good catch, and even water corpses washed ashore or found near the shore are surprisingly considered a positive sign and are often buried respectfully in the village cemetery.

Among Ninigi's companions on the way to Earth are five kami, who are considered to be the ancestors of five different Japanese family clans and who also each represent a profession: Hatmaker, Shieldmaker, Metalworker, Weaver and Jewelmaker. That they come to earth with Ninigi explains not only why these professions are common among people, but also why each family traditionally practiced the respective profession. Likewise, Hoderi's oath that his descendants would serve those of his brother Hoori is a legitimization for the role of the family clan tracing back to Hoderi in the empire.

ROLE AND (PSEUDO) HISTORI-
CITY OF THE TENNŌ

The role of the imperial house in Japan is to a large extent legitimized mythologically. Der mythologische erste Tennō (Titel des japanischen Kaisers; wörtlich „Sohn des Himmels") ist demnach der Ururururenkel (d. h. Nachfahre in fünfter Generation) der Amaterasu, wodurch das Bild vermittelt wird, dass die kaiserliche Familie in direkter Linie von ihr abstammt.

The sword captured by Susanoo (Kusanagi no Tsurugi), the necklace of Amaterasu (Yasakani no Magatama) and the mirror placed in front of Amaterasu's cave (Yata no Kagami) were, according to legend, given to Ninigi by Amaterasu on his way to earth and bequeathed by him to his descendants. They are called the three imperial insignia of Japan (Sanshu no Jingi, literally "three sacred treasures") and are said to be still in the possession of the imperial family today, which also legitimizes their power.

The part of the recorded chronicle of Japan that can be called mythological does not end with the age of the kami, but continues for many years through Japanese history, ending, depending on the historical view, in the first century B.C. or even as late as the sixth century A.D. Not only is the Jinmu-Tennō most likely mythological, but it is also assumed of his eight successors that they did not really live in the mythologically described form. Whether they existed at all, and whether the surviving dates of their birth, death, and reign are correct, is highly questionable. Only for the existence of the tenth Japanese emperor, the Sujin-Tennō, who took the reign in 97 BC, is there historical evidence. Nevertheless, he and some of his successors are also often referred to as "legendary" because the evidence, while suggesting their existence, is not strong enough to establish their historicity unequivocally.

The 15th emperor, Ōjin-Tennō, who ascended the throne in 270 AD, is considered by some historians to be the first Tennō, whose existence-despite still inconclusive evidence-is highly probable. The historicity of some of his successors is supported by the fact that they probably coincide with the Japanese rulers mentioned in Chinese records, who are referred to there as the "Five Kings of Wa" and sent envoys to China to be recognized by the emperor there. All successors to the throne from the 29th emperor, Kinmei-Tennō, who ruled from 539 to 571, are historically attested. This applies both to their existence per se and to the dates of their birth, accession, and death.

It is believed that in the history of recording Japanese myths, the original narrative text was occasionally altered or manipulated for politically motivated reasons in order to secure the position of the imperial family. Among other things, the special position often given to the historical province of Yamato, as well as its frequent mention as a synonym for all of Japan, was probably constructed after the fact because the imperial family originated there.

It is also quite possible that the sword Ōkuninushi receives from Susanoo and with which he defeats his brothers and secures his rule over the earth for the time being is the Kusanagi no Tsurugi captured by him. But since this must come into the possession of the imperial family in order to legitimize their power, the myth was modified, presumably by order of a Tennō, so that Amaterasu initially keeps the Kusanagi no Tsurugi with her and later gives it to Ninigi along the way. The sword bequeathed to Ōkuninushi was renamed to an unnamed "Sword of Life." In other versions, it is instead a spear or is not mentioned at all.

Contrary to popular belief, however, it is not true that the Tennō himself was once believed by the

Japanese people to be a kami in human form. While he is considered a human being descended from the kami, he is not otherwise perceived to have anything super-natural or non-human about him. Thus, when the United States called upon the 124th Tennō, Hirohito, after World War II to publicly acknowledge that he was human, this did not change the opinion of the general Japanese population toward their head of state, contrary to the American view.

MOTIFS

A defining motif of Japanese mythology is the personality of the kami, which is usually very human in appearance. They show human emotions, often react all too humanly to external circumstances or to the behavior of others, they occasionally make mistakes, and they behave strongly or weakly in various kinds of situations. In somewhat more general terms, they think, act, and react in ways that are understandable to humans. However, as already mentioned, this is the rule case, which is not without exceptions.

In more isolated cases, the behavior of some kami defies human understanding. The earliest example is Izanami in the underworld. It is understandable that she does not want to be seen by her brother and partner in her condition; her subsequent reaction, on the other hand, seems disproportionately exaggerated at best and completely incomprehensible at worst. Such occurrences are not all that frequent, but they are particularly noticeable every time.

Another motif that Japanese mythology contains - or, more precisely, often does not contain - is the concept of good and evil. For the most part, it is conspicuously absent. There are kami, as well as other beings and also deeds, that clearly have negative connotations, but the state that prevails most of the time is one of ambivalence.

There is a certain idea of morality, but it is only very vaguely defined. At points where something is clearly to be perceived by the observer as good or evil, as just or unjust, not only do the kami appear rather impassive, but also the narrative of the text itself rarely takes sides and rarely specifies how the situation should be judged morally. Of course, there are exceptions, such as the extreme case of Susanoo's misdeeds, which are unanimously condemned by the kami and where the narrative of the text also makes it unmistakably clear that these are clearly evil deeds.

Certain objects also appear more frequently as motifs. A good example is the Totsuka no Tsurugi (literally "ten-handed sword"). When a sword is mentioned, it always happens that it is exactly such a sword. The sword with which Izanagi kills his son Kagutsuchi and cuts up his body, for example, is a Totsuka no Tsurugi. It is later named Itsu no Ohabari and even appears as a living, talking being or full-fledged kami. The contest between Amaterasu and Susanoo involved another unnamed Totsuka no Tsurugi, and the sword Susanoo uses to strike down Orochi is also of this type (as opposed to the legendary Kusanagi no Tsurugi he finds in the monster's body).

When Takemikazuchi demands that Ōkuninushi hand over the reigns after his arrival on earth, he also sits on a Totsuka no Tsurugi with the proper name Futsu Mitama no Tsurugi, which he himself had previously stuck into the ground. The same sword later, through Takemikazuchi's intervention, comes in a roundabout way into the hands of the future Jinmu-Tennō, Kamu-yamato Iware-biko, whom it helps to win a battle in the Kumano region.

Finally, it cannot be ignored that incest is also a recurring motif. Some kami marry their family members, often their immediate siblings, and give birth to offspring with them. In the textual record, this is not commented on as unusual or wrong, and the offspring do not exhibit any associated consequences. For example, the state Hiruko is in at birth is attributed to the wedding ritual gone wrong, not to the kinship relationship of his parents. Moreover, the children who follow him do not seem to be affected by the same problems. Probably one of the most obvious and obvious reasons for this is that despite their predominantly human-like personalities, the kami are not to be equated with humans, and thus neither the negative

reputation or taboo nor the consequences of incest ne-
cessarily apply to them.

But even beyond that, there are further reasons for
the increased occurrence. First, marriages between
half-siblings were not uncommon in the imperial family until about the sixth century; second, the word
imo (modern reading: imōto), which nowadays almost
always stands for "younger sister," can also mean
"wife" in ancient Japanese, which is why some suppo-
sed incest cases in Japanese mythology may not really
mean siblings.

Source

KOJIKI

The two most important literary works considered to be sources of Japanese mythology are the Kojiki (literally. "Record of Ancient Incidents") and the Nihon Shoki (literally. "Written Chronicle of Japan"). Both works begin with the mythological origin of the world, and their narrative extends to the first millennium AD. In addition, they have in common that, although they are not considered completely reliable historical sources, they are nevertheless considered important by historians and archaeologists because of the descriptions of ancient Japan they contain.

When speaking of different versions of a mythological tale, this usually refers to the version in the Kojiki and the one in the Nihon shoki. Sometimes only details of an otherwise identical narrative differ between the two works, but often the differences are greater and the two versions contradict each other. Such a contradiction can occur even within the same work and stems from the fact that two different traditions have met and an attempt has been made to combine them into one and the same event, although they originally stood independently for themselves. Also, the names of some kami differ between kojiki and nihon shoki; in such cases, it is often clear from the context that the same kami is being referred to.

The Kojiki is the oldest surviving literary work in Japan. It is important to note that the content of the entire text was not taken directly from other, older records and written narratives, but was dictated orally by a single person.

The imperial family and other family clans ruling at various times made various records of their genealogies and various anecdotes concerning their origins and past even before the Kojiki came into being. This practice probably began in the sixth century A.D. Because contradictions sometimes occurred, the 40th emperor, Tenmu, ordered a closer inspection and revision of the records during his reign in order to clear up these contradictions as well as eliminate the errors that had crept in over time. At the same time, however, he intended to combine several ruling families from the past into a single large, unbroken family, as well as to establish a mythological legitimation for the rule of this family and for the positions of the members of other families within the ruling system.

A reciter named Hieda no Are (whether he was a man or a woman is not known and cannot be identified from the name) was assigned to memorize the result of this revision. Are was one of Tenmu-Tennō's confidants, possessed, according to tradition, an exceptionally good memory, and came from a family whose lineage was said to go back to Ame no Uzume. It was not until 711, 25 years after the end of the Tenmu-Tennō's reign, that the 43rd empress, Genmei, ordered it to be written down. The Kojiki was completed around the year 712 at her court by the scribe Ō no Yasumaro. The content is based on the narrative reproduced by Are.

The text of the Kojiki is divided into three parts, preceded by a brief preface by Ō no Yasumaro, in which he describes the history of the work's creation and explains its structure and some of its written characteristics. The first part ranges from the beginning of Heaven and Earth and the Koto Amatsukami to the birth of the Jinmu-Tennō. The second part describes the course of the imperial family through the period of the first 15 emperors from the Jinmu-Tennō to the Ōjin-Tennō. The third part describes the further course of the family history from the Nintoku-Tennō to the 33rd empress, Suiko-Tennō.

NIHON SHOKI

The Nihon shoki is the second oldest surviving literary work in Japan and also the first of six chronicles of Japanese mythology and history written at the imperial court in the eighth and ninth centuries, all of which cover a different time period. It differs from the Kojiki in many ways: While the Kojiki, written in Sino-Japanese, was intended for readers within Japan, the Nihon shoki, written in classical Chinese, was intended as a national chronicle that could be presented to other peoples.

The Kojiki is also based on sources passed on within the imperial family, whereas the Nihon shoki also draws its information from outside sources. Furthermore, the historical information in the Nihon shoki is considered to be closer to actual reality. This is in stark contrast to the Kojiki, which values a coherent, unbroken mythological narrative thread over a precise orientation to historical facts. Finally, the two works differ in that the Nihon shoki is more detailed in the historical aspect than the Kojiki, which tends to simplify historical events and embellish them with myths. However, it omits some mythological narratives, presumably because they are not relevant enough to the historical context of the work.

Unlike the three sections of the Kojiki (dividing a text into three parts, an "upper," a "middle," and a "lower," is common in classical Japanese literature), the Nihon shoki consists of 30 chapters. Only the first two tell of the age of kami, and already the third begins with the Jinmu-Tennō. The further chapters reach up to the 41st empress, Jinō-Tennō, whereby not always a single chapter is dedicated to each Tennō, since occasionally two or three of them are combined in a common chapter and the time of the Tenmu-Tennō even stretches over two chapters, which could be related to its importance for the emergence of the Kojiki.

No chapter at all is devoted to the 39th emperor, Kōbun-Tenno, since his reign lasted only a few months. A special case occurs relatively early in the text: After the third chapter, which deals with the first emperor, the nearly five-century period (581 to 98 BCE) from the second to the ninth emperor is summarized in a single chapter, in which only very rough outline data on their lives and reigns are enumerated. This could be related to the fact that they are all considered to be absolutely mythological and not attested in any way. Although this is also true for the Jinmu-Tennō, this one, in contrast to his successors called kesshi hachidai (literally "eight emperors without chronicles"), is too important. Only the Sujin-Tennō, which is at the same time the first Tennō with historical evidence, gets its own chapter again.

The chapters do not document almost exclusively the experiences of the imperial family, as in the Kojiki, but also include broader accounts of Japan's fortunes during their reigns. The emperors are not portrayed exclusively in heroic terms; just as the virtues of the good emperors are reported, so too are the misdeeds of the worse emperors. Japan's contact with foreign countries is also documented. The history of the origin of the Kojiki is also included in the Nihon shoki. For the period from 661 to 697, it is considered a historically accurate document; the rest of the work is considered to have varying degrees of veracity.

Other mythologies within Japan

BUDDHIST-SHINTŌIST SYNCRE-TISM

After the establishment of Buddhism in Japan, the Shinbutsu-konkō (literally "Kami-Buddha mixture"), the union of Shintō with Buddhism imported from China, began. Thus, in some respects, a hybrid of elements of Buddhism and Shintō emerged. The technical term for such a mixture is syncretism. One phenomenon of this combination in some places was the so-called shrine temples made up of Shintō shrines and Buddhist temples, or the popularization of shrine monks who were present as Buddhist monks in most Shintō shrines. Also, although the shinbutsu-bunri ("literally kami Buddha division") in the 19th century again caused a separation as well as a general reduction of Buddhist influence in Japan, some influences of the shinbutsu-konkō are still present today. These include the association of various kami from Shintō mythology with Buddhist deities. These were either regarded as identical with the respective deities worshipped in Buddhism or as other incarnations or manifestations of them.

One of the best-known examples of this is that four of the Buddhist "seven gods of fortune" (Jap. Shichifukujin) are still associated with particular kami. Ebisu, god of fishermen and fishing, is usually considered identical to Hiruko, the first son of Izanagi and Izanami, who, after being abandoned by them at sea, was found by the first people living in Japan who took care of him. After surviving some hardships, his deformities present at birth are said to have healed, so he is still depicted with a slightly stooped posture, but with an eye-catching smile.

Other traditions also exist according to which Ebisu is identical with Kotoshironushi, one of the sons of Ōkuninushi. Daikokuten, god of cuisine, wealth and fertility, is considered identical to Ōkuninushi, as both are associated with the same place in Japan and are often depicted as carrying a sack on their backs and accompanied by a mouse. There are also similarities in their spelling. Benzaiten, goddess of art, music and eloquence, is considered the essence of Ugajin, kami of harvest and fertility. She is often depicted with his image above her head. Bishamonten, god of the fortunes of war, is associated with Hachiman, the Ōjin-Tennō who became kami after his death. Hachiman is also associated with success in battles.

MYTHOLOGY OF THE AINU

The Ainu are the indigenous people of the northernmost Japanese island of Hokkaidō and the Tōhoku region on the main island of Honshū. In addition, they are also native to some areas in the east of present-day Russia. They belong to a different ethnic group than the present-day Japanese and have their own language unrelated to Japanese. Historically, they have often been in conflict with the Japanese, who, like many indigenous peoples around the world, have oppressed them.

It is only since 2008 that they have been recognized in Japan as an indigenous people with their own culture. Since many Ainu in the past and even today live isolated from the Japanese population, it is hardly surprising that they also have their own mythology. Not as much is known about this as about the Japanese, which is partly due to the fact that the Ainu, like the Japanese, did not have a writing system for a long time, and myths were transmitted purely orally. Works such as the Kojiki and the Nihon shoki did not and do not exist among the Ainu. Due to the oppression and violence that the Ainu experienced from the Japanese, their population declined, so that their folk beliefs are hardly practiced today, which also makes it difficult to study them.

The mythology of the Ainu has similarities with the Japanese, for example, there is talk of spiritual, spiritual beings, who are called Kamuy in the language of the Ainu. Not only the name shows similarities with the Japanese term kami. Also the characteristics of the Kamuy resemble these, are however not identical. In addition, one version of the Ainu creation myth mentions a celestial couple named Ae Oyna Kamuy and Turesh who come to earth and whose son is the first Ainu. The fact that Ae Oyna Kamuy carries a spear is a striking parallel to Izanagi and Izanami.

A significant component of Ainu mythology not found in Japanese mythology is the important role of the bear, which is reflected in a bear cult, that is, the ritual worship of bears. It is often told of how the Kamuy appear in bear form in the world of humans and take their true form only in their own world. In one version of the Ainu creation myth, the bear is also mentioned as the original ancestor of the Ainu, presumably because the Ainu have more pronounced body hair than other peoples.

FOLK TALES AND URBAN LE-GENDS

Also worth mentioning are the folk tales and urban legends that are widespread in Japan. These are often not clearly distinguishable from the actual mythology. They usually do not include depictions of the kami, but do incorporate certain symbolism or other elements established by Japanese mythology. For example, the story of Momotarō is about a boy who hatches from a peach and is raised as a son by a childless couple. The important role of the peach in Japanese perception is related to its role in Izanagi's escape from the underworld, as described above.

The story of Urashima Tarō tells of the young fisherman of the same name who rescues a turtle from a group of other children who are torturing it for fun. It turns out that the turtle is actually the princess of a kingdom lying under the sea, and as a reward for the rescue he is invited by her to her palace the next day. There she confronts him in human form and the two marry. After spending, from his own point of view, only a few days with her, he becomes homesick and wants to return to his homeland. The princess hesitantly agrees and gives him a casket to take with him, but at the same time warns him never to open it.

Once ashore, he quickly discovers that his family, his friends, and all the other people he knew are no longer there, and instead there are people living in his house and hometown who are strangers to him. When he asks a passing man if he has heard of a young man named Urashima Tarō, the man replies that the boy disappeared into the sea hundreds of years ago.

Horrified and saddened by the fact that he has been absent for several hundred years, he opens the casket. As a result, he suddenly begins to age and turns into an old man with a long white beard. The casket contained all the years of his life that he had spent in the underwater palace. By enclosing them, he was spared their effects, and by opening them, they took effect with rapid speed. At the bottom of the casket he finds a feather. He takes it, is transformed by it into a crane and flies away.

Despite some differences, clear parallels can be seen with the mythological story of Hoori. Both Hoori and Urashima Tarō, as fishermen, marry a woman who comes from a world under the sea and receive a super-natural object from her. Both are explicitly warned by their wives not to do something specific: Hoori is not to look at Toyotama-hime during the birth, and Urashima Tarō is not to open the casket. However, due to their curiosity, both defy their respective requests and have to bear the consequences of their actions:

Hoori loses his mate and Urashima Tarō loses his youth or lifetime. Also, the king of the sea who appears in the story, Ryūjin, is considered synonymous with Watatsumi in some traditions. Furthermore, it is believed that the name of the story, and perhaps even its entire existence, stems from the fact that in the 14th chapter of the Nihon Shoki, long after the tale of Hoori, it is mentioned in passing that a boy named Urashima visited the realm of Watatsumi and saw wondrous things there.

Conversely, characters from Japanese folk tales also have an influence on the understanding of the mythology. Sarutahiko was depicted for a long time in artistic representations as resembling a monkey, due to its name and also because its face and rump are described as red. However, the growing popularity of the tengu, winged mythical creatures with long noses that are the subject of many folk tales, ensured that Sarutahiko, who also possesses an exceptionally long nose, was over time increasingly depicted with an external appearance resembling a tengu.